How to Make
CREPE PAPER
FLOWERS

ℋow to make
CREPE PAPER FLOWERS

SECOND EDITION

Contents

National Flowers

Alaska—Forget-me-not
Canada—Maple Leaf
China—Narcissus
Egypt—Lotus
England—Rose
France—Fleur-de-lis
Germany—Cornflower
Greece—Violet
India—Lotus
Ireland—Shamrock

Italy—White Lily
Japan—Chrysanthemum
Mexico—Cactus
Persia—Rose
Scotland—Thistle
Spain—Pomegranate
Switzerland—Edelweiss
United States—Goldenrod
Wales—Leek

Flowers of the Months

January—Snowdrop
February—Primrose
March—Violet
April—Daisy
May—Hawthorn or Apple
  Blossom
June—Rose

July—Poppy
August—Water Lily
September—Morning Glory or
  Goldenrod
October—Aster
November—Chrysanthemum
December—Holly

State Flowers

Alabama—Goldenrod
Arizona—Sahuaro Cactus
Arkansas—Apple Blossom
California—Golden Poppy
Colorado—Columbine
Connecticut—Mountain Laurel
Delaware—Peach Blossom
Florida—Orange Blossom
Georgia—Cherokee Rose
Idaho—Syringa
Illinois—Wood Violet
Indiana—Carnation
Iowa—Wild Rose
Kansas—Sunflower
Kentucky—Trumpet Vine
Louisiana—Magnolia
Maine—Pine Cone and Tassel
Maryland—Black-Eyed Susan
Massachusetts—Mayflower
Michigan—Apple Blossom
Minnesota—Moccasin Flower
Mississippi—Magnolia
Missouri—Hawthorn
Montana—Bitter Root

Nebraska—Goldenrod
Nevada—Sagebrush
New Hampshire—Purple Lilac
New Jersey—Violet
New Mexico—Cactus
New York—Rose
North Carolina—Goldenrod
North Dakota—Wild Prairie Rose
Ohio—Scarlet Carnation
Oklahoma—Mistletoe
Oregon—Oregon Grape
Pennsylvania—(No choice)
Rhode Island—Violet
South Carolina—Yellow Jessamine
South Dakota—Pasque Flower
Tennessee—Passion Flower
Texas—Bluebonnet
Utah—Sego Lily
Vermont—Red Clover
Virginia—American Dogwood
Washington—Rhododendron
West Virginia—Rhododendron
Wisconsin—Violet
Wyoming—Indian Paintbush

How to Make Crepe Paper Flowers

EVERYONE loves flowers, and when it is impossible to obtain natural ones, flowers of crepe paper can be easily made; flowers so beautiful, so perfect in form and color that only by touching them can you distinguish that they are not real. And crepe paper flowers will last and retain their original beauty and freshness for weeks and for months when real flowers fade in a few short hours.

Crepe Paper Flower Making is one of the most fascinating of all Dennison crafts. It affords a delightful diversion to those who seek an inexpensive means of giving expression to their creative instinct, and to those who desire to turn their skill into money making it offers many opportunities.

There are instructions in this book for 24 different flowers, as well as directions for waxing flowers. You will also find on page 34 the approximate amount of materials required, and the cost of making the various flowers in quantities. The cost is approximated without taking into consideration that often only a very small part of a fold of crepe paper of a certain color is required for the quantity of flowers specified, so that the actual cost of making should, in many instances, be less than estimated.

All of the flowers for which instructions are given were copied from Nature. But Nature herself rarely makes two flowers exactly alike and there are often several varieties of the same flower. If any of the flowers shown differ from those with which you are familiar do not conclude that the patterns are wrong but rather that Nature varies. Sometimes, too, slight variations from actual flowers are necessary to make the flower simpler to construct or more substantial and usable.

The patterns furnished with this book were originally made from the natural flowers and are as nearly perfect as it is possible to make them. When you are making flowers, if possible use two natural ones as guides, one to take apart and the other to use as a study.

Instructions and patterns for flowers not contained in this book may be obtained either in the "Home Course of Flower Making" which is described elsewhere in this book or by writing the Service Bureau at the nearest Dennison Store.

Stationers, department stores and many drug stores carry a full line of Dennison Goods and in many shops instructions are given without charge.

Buy Dennison Goods from your local dealer

Sweet Pea

A list of materials required is on page 34

SWEET PEAS may be made in a great variety of colors (see page 36); the petals sometimes being made of two different shades of the same color. They may be made either with circular petals or with lobed petals. For the calyx, leaves and stem wrapping use No. 45 Moss Green Crepe Paper, No. 1 spool wire for the flower stem, and No. 9 wire for the foliage stem.

Circular Petals—Cut two petals and one calyx for each flower, using patterns Nos. 1 and 2. (Gen. Instr. No. 1, page 31.) Flute the two opposite edges of the circular petals. (Gen. Instr. No. 2.) Place two petals together so that the fluted edges of the top petal are 1/4 inch lower than those of the under petal. (Fig. 1.) Fold upward the two bottom edges so that the four edges will be 1/4 inch apart. (Fig. 2.) Place the end of a 10-inch strip of spool wire along the inside of the fold and gather the petals closely on the wire. (Fig. 3.) Twist the wire underneath to hold the gathers in place. (Fig. 4.) Paste the calyx around the base of the flower, points upward, placing it high enough to cover the gathers neatly, and pressing the lower part against the stem wire.

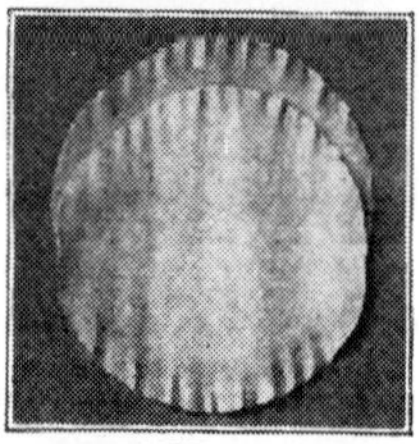

Stem—Cut *across the grain* a strip of No. 45 Moss Green Crepe Paper, 1/2 inch wide, and wrap the stem, starting close up under the base. (Gen. Instr. No. 3.)

Cup the outside petal inward and the next one outward. (Gen. Instr. No. 4.) Press forward the two ends that form the center so that they stand out. (Fig. 8.)

Foliage—If foliage is desired, use leaf pattern No. 3 and make separate sprays using No. 9 wire for the stem. Place the leaves 1 1/2 inches apart on opposite sides of the stem, or they may be placed in twos similar to Fig. 5. (Gen. Instr. No. 5.)

Fig. 1

Fig. 2

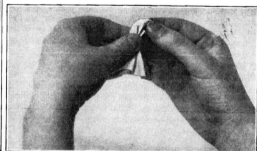

Fig. 8

Fig. 6. Pulling the Top of the Center over toward the Closed Side

Attractive tendrils are made by wrapping a 10-inch strip of green spool wire tightly and closely around a steel knitting needle. Slip the twisted wire off the needle, stretch and bend it slightly and insert a straight end in the stem wrapping with the leaves.

Lobed Petals—Cut petals from patterns Nos. 4 and 5. Flute the top and bottom edges. (Gen. Instr. No. 2.)

Center—Stretch a strip of paper slightly and cut a 3-inch square. Fold diagonally twice. One-half inch below the double folded center point gather and pull the top over toward the closed side. (Fig. 6.)

Place the center at the lower center of the inside petal and add the outside petal. (Fig. 7.) Fasten all together at the end of a 10-inch strip of spool wire. (Gen. Instr. No. 6a.) Add calyx and wrap stem as instructed for circular petal Sweet Pea. Cup the outside petals inward and the inside petals outward. (Fig. 9.)

Shaping—After the flower is completed, it is sometimes necessary to reshape it by fluting the edges, recupping the petals, and sometimes the inside petals of both the circular and lobed petal Sweet Pea may be improved by curling the top edges forward over a knitting needle.

Both the flower stem and foliage stem should be slightly bent so that they will droop gracefully and not appear stiff.

Two Shades—When two shades are used in a Sweet Pea, there is no regular rule for placing the light or the darker shade. It is permissible to vary the shading, as you will find it varies in the natural flower. Sometimes the darker shade is used in the center of the lobed petal Sweet Pea with a dark outside and a light inside petal. Sometimes the light center is used with a light inside and a dark outside petal, and so on.

Fig. 3

Fig. 4

Fig. 7.   Putting the Center and Petals Together

Fig. 5   Fig. 9

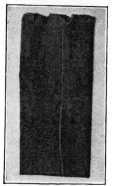

Fig. 15

Fig. 11

Jonquil

A list of materials required is on page 34

JONQUILS may be made of two shades, No. 63 Dark Amber for the pistil and center tube and No. 61 Light Amber for the petals; or all one color, No. 62 Canary. Use No. 70 Sand for the sheath, No. 45 Moss Green for the leaves and stem wrapping, with spool wire and No. 9 wire.

Pistil—Cut *across the grain* a strip ½ inch wide by 2 inches long. Stretch fully. Fold one narrow edge over about ⅛ inch, making it a little thicker than the balance of the rolled strip, and starting at this folded end, roll the strip diagonally downward into a tight twist. (Fig. 10.)

Tube—Using pattern No. 6 cut out the tube (Gen. Instr. No. 1, page 31) and flute each of the six scallops once. (Gen. Instr. No. 2.) Paste the two opposite straight edges together, one on top of the other. (Fig. 11.) Place the pistil in the center of the tube with the bud end slightly below the edge, and gather the tube 1 inch up from the bottom. Place a finger in the center and press into tube shape.

Petals—Using pattern No. 7, cut two strips of three petals each for each flower. Full the first three-petal strip around the tube evenly, the tips of the petals ¼ inch higher than the tube. (Fig. 12.) Full the other three petals around the outside between and at the same height as the first three. Fasten all together with a 10-inch strip of spool wire. (Fig. 13.) (Gen. Instr. No. 6a.)

Sheath—Using pattern No. 8 cut one sheath for each Jonquil. Crush between the fingers, then draw it out slightly, giving the appearance of a dried petal. (Fig. 14.)

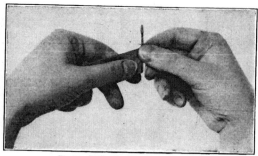

Fig. 12

Fig. 10. Rolling the Crepe Paper into a Pistil

Stem—Begin the stem wrapping, using an inch wide strip of the green crepe paper. (Gen. Instr. No. 3.) One inch below the base of the flower insert the sheath, about ½ inch being enclosed in the wrapping. (Gen. Instr. No. 5.) Add two 12-inch No. 9 wires (Gen. Instr. No. 7) to lengthen the stem. Insert two leaves (pattern No. 9) on opposite sides and about 8 inches down the stem. Complete the stem wrapping to the end.

Shaping—Draw the petals away from the center, making them appear at right angles to the base. Cup them inward and bend the flower forward one inch from the base, the sheath to the back. (Gen. Instr. No. 4.) (Fig. 15.)

Fig. 17

Daffodil

DAFFODILS are made in the same colors and exactly like Jonquils with the exception of the centers. Instead of the pistil and tube, a double or cluster center is made of a strip of No. 63 Dark Amber Crepe Paper, cut *across the grain* 3 inches wide and 15 inches long. Flute one long edge, several thicknesses at a time, to avoid the danger of tearing. (Gen. Instr. No. 2.) Gather the strip 1 inch up from the unfluted edge and gradually gather and roll it into tube shape. Hold the strip closely at the base while gathering and rolling, and roll it only slightly or it will be too close and tight. If the inside rises above the outer edges, loosen the hold at the base slightly and press down from the top with the palm of the hand. Complete the same as the Jonquil. (Figs. 16 and 17.)

Fig. 14

Fig. 16   Forming the Daffodil Center

Fig. 13

Tulip

A list of materials required is on page 34

TULIPS may be with single or with double petals, both being cut from the same pattern. For colors, and combination of colors, see page 36.

Center—Make a ball ½ inch in diameter, of crepe paper crumpled in the hand. Stretch over it a 2½-inch square of No. 41 or 45 Green Crepe Paper, and pinch together underneath. Cut a strip of No. 12 Black Crepe Paper 2 inches wide. Cut a fine fringe 1 inch deep. (Gen. Instr. No. 12, page 33.) Full about 3 inches of the strip around the ball, the top of the fringe extending ¾ of an inch above the ball. Fasten with spool wire. (Fig. 18.)

Petals—Cut six single petals (pattern No. 10) (Gen. Instr. No. 1), or for double petals first paste together evenly along one edge two strips of crepe paper, 4 inches wide by 11 inches long, and when cutting place the top or rounded end of the pattern at the pasted edge. Cup the petals ⅔ down from the top. (Gen. Instr. No. 4.) Full three petals around the center, their tops extending 1¼ inches above the top of the fringe and the sides overlapping equally. (Figs. 19 and 20.) Arrange the other three petals in another row between the first three. Fasten with a 10-inch strip of spool wire. (Gen. Instr. No. 6a.) Paste the three outside petals together at the lower sides.

Stem—For a double wrapping of the stem, use a ½ inch wide strip of No. 45 Moss Green Crepe Paper. (Gen. Instr. No. 3.) Two inches down the stem add two 9-inch No. 9 wires (Gen. Instr. No. 7) and continue the wrapping to the end. Wrap the stem a second time with the ½ inch wide strip and, 9 inches down, insert two leaves (pattern No. 11) on opposite sides of the stem. (Gen. Instr. No. 5.)

Shaping—Place the finger inside of the flower and press down around the center to make a shorter and more naturally shaped tulip.

Fig. 18

Fig. 19

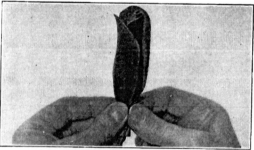

Fig. 20. Three Single Petals Placed

Flanders Poppy

A list of materials required is on page 34

THE Flanders Poppy is usually made of No. 84
Flame Crepe Paper, although it may be made in
other colors. (See page 36.) Use No. 45 Moss Green
Crepe Paper for the center, leaves and stem wrapping,
and No. 12 Black for the fringe; with spool wire and, if
a long stem with leaves is desired, No. 9 wire.

Center—Make a ball ¼ inch in diameter of crumpled
crepe paper and stretch over it smoothly a 2-inch square
of No. 45 Moss Green Crepe Paper. Pinch together underneath. *Cut across the grain* a 1½ inch wide strip of
No. 12 Black and of No. 45 Moss Green Crepe Paper.
Stretch the strips, fold together *with the grain*, and cut
a fine fringe along one edge ½ inch deep. (Gen. Instr.
No. 12, page 33.) Place a strip of the double fringe—
about one inch—around the ball, the top of the fringe
about ⅜ inch above the ball. Fasten with a 6-inch
strip of spool wire (Gen. Instr. No. 6a), leaving a single
wire for the stem. (Fig. 21.)

Petals—Cut two petals for each flower, using pattern
No. 1. (Gen. Instr. No. 1.) If preferred, they may be cut
larger or smaller than the pattern. Flute two opposite
edges of the petals. (Gen. Instr. No. 2.) Place one on top
of the other, the sheen side up, no two fluted edges together. Make an opening in the center of the petals by
first folding them in half and again in half, without
creasing, and clipping off the center point. (Figs. 22 and
23.) Brush a little paste on the center of the top petal
(Fig. 23) and draw the stem wire down through the
opening, forcing the base of the ball through also, being
careful not to make an ugly tear. Press the petals upward and wrap the stem with a ½ inch wide strip of
No. 45 Moss Green Crepe Paper, starting high enough
up to cover the opening in the center. (Gen. Instr. No.
3.) (Fig. 24.)

If a long stem is desired, add two No. 9 wires each 10
inches long (Gen. Instr. No. 7), and insert a leaf (pattern No. 13) three inches down the stem (Gen. Instr.
Nos. 1 and 5), and two other leaves on opposite sides
three inches apart.

Fig. 21

Fig. 22

Fig. 23

Fig. 24 Wrapping Base and Stem

Fig. 25

Fig. 26

Fig. 27

Red Poppy

A list of materials required is on page 34

RED Poppies are made with single petals or a strip of petals. Use No. 81 Red Crepe Paper for the petals, No. 45 Moss Green for the center ball, fringe, leaves and stem wrapping, No. 12 Black for the center fringe; with spool wire and No. 9 wire.

Center—Make a ball ½ inch in diameter by crumpling some green crepe paper in the hand and stretching over it a 2½-inch square of the green crepe paper. Pinch together underneath. (Fig. 25.) Cut a strip each of No. 45 Moss Green and No. 12 Black Crepe Paper, 1½ inches wide by 6 inches long, and make a double fringe 1 inch deep. (Gen. Instr. No. 12, page 33.) (Fig. 26.) Gather this double fringe around the ball, the top of the fringe extending ½ inch above the ball, and fasten with a 5-inch strip of spool wire. (Gen. Instr. No. 6a.) (Fig. 27.) Dennison's ready-made poppy stamens may be used in place of the fringed crepe.

Petals—Cut four single petals for each flower (pattern No. 12) and flute the top edges. (Gen. Instr. Nos. 1 and 2.) Cup the petals, the sheen side to the inside. (Gen. Instr. No. 4.) Full the petals evenly around the center, sheen side next to the center, the top of the petals 1½ inches above the top of the fringe. (Fig. 28.) Fasten tightly with a 6-inch piece of spool wire. (Gen. Instr. No. 6a.)

Stem and Leaves—Wrap the stem with a ¾ inch wide strip of No. 45 Moss Green Crepe Paper (Gen. Instr. No. 3), inserting the first leaf, cut from pattern No. 13, four inches down the stem (Gen. Instr. No. 5), and one or two other leaves two inches apart on opposite sides of the stem. Add three No. 9 wires, to make the stem about 18 inches long. (Gen. Instr. No. 7.)

Shaping—The petals may be held together with a little paste at the lower side edges. Curl the leaves slightly over a blade away from the stem. (Gen. Instr. No. 9a.)

Fig. 28. Placing the Third Petal

Daisies

A list of materials required is on page 34

THE centers of the White Daisy and the Marguerite are made with No. 63 Dark Amber, and the Black-Eyed Susan with No. 72 Brown and No. 12 Black Crepe Paper. The petals of the White Daisy are made with No. 11 White, the Black-Eyed Susan with No. 63 Dark Amber, and the Marguerite with No. 61 Light Amber Crepe Paper. No. 45 Moss Green is used for all leaves and stem wrapping.

Fig. 33

Centers—The Daisy and Marguerite are made exactly the same—the difference is in the color of the petals. Make a ball slightly less than ½ inch in diameter. Stretch over it a 2-inch square of No. 63 Dark Amber Crepe Paper, and pinch together underneath. Flatten the ball by pressing against some hard surface. (Fig. 29.)

For the Black-Eyed Susan center, *cut across the grain,* a strip each of No. 12 Black and No. 72 Brown Crepe Paper, 1½ inches wide by 7 inches long. Roll the two strips together evenly, and fasten with paste. Clip off one end into cone shape, ½ inch down. (Fig. 30.)

Fig. 32

Petals—With petal pattern No. 14 cut strips of 12 or more petals. (Gen. Instr. Nos. 1 and 8, pages 31 and 33.) Full the petals evenly around the center ⅝ inch up from the bottom edge, or further up if a smaller flower is desired. (Fig. 31.) Fasten with a 10-inch strip of spool wire. (Gen. Instr. No. 6a.) Wrap the stem with a ½-inch strip of No. 45 Moss Green Crepe Paper (Gen. Instr. No. 3) and add 2 or 3 No. 9 wires as needed to strengthen and lengthen the stem to 15 inches. (Gen. Instr. No. 7.) Insert leaves at unequal distances apart along the stem, using pattern No. 15 for the Daisy and Marguerite leaves (Fig. 32), and No. 16 for the Black-Eyed Susan. (Fig. 33.) (Gen. Instr. No. 5.)

Fig. 29

Fig. 31.   Arranging the Petals Around the Center

Fig. 30

Pond Lily

A list of materials required is on page 34

Fig. 34a

Fig. 34b

Fig. 36

SEE page 36 for the colors in which Pond Lilies may be made. No. 63 Dark Amber is used in the center, No. 41 Apple Green on the inside of calyx and in the center, No. 46 Leaf Green on the outside of calyx, for the stem wrapping, and for the leaf; with No. 9 wire.

Center—Cut *across the grain* a strip of amber and of apple green crepe paper 1 inch wide. Stretch and cut into 5-inch lengths. Twist the two colors together and ⅜ inch from either side of the center bend the strips down and press tightly. (Fig. 34a.) Cut a 2 inch wide strip of amber crepe paper. Stretch and fold several times *with the grain*. Cut into a pointed fringe ⅝ inch deep. Curl this fringe over a blade (Gen. Instr. No. 9a, page 33) and cut into 5-inch lengths. Gather a strip around the pistil, curled ends inward, the ends ¼ inch above the top of the pistil. Gather a second strip around ¼ inch higher than the first row, curled ends outward. Fasten with paste. (Fig. 34b.)

Calyx—Cut strips of apple green and leaf green crepe paper 4 inches wide and 4¼ inches long. Brush one edge with paste and place the other strip on top evenly. Fold the double strip in the center *with the grain* twice and cut four calyxes in a strip (pattern No. 24), the rounded ends of the pattern to the pasted edge. (Gen. Instr. Nos. 1 and 8.) Cup near the top, the light green to the inside. (Gen. Instr. No. 4.)

Petals—Cut a strip of 30 petals using pattern No. 25. With the sheen side of the paper toward you, cup the first 12 petals deeply near the top and cup the balance gradually less and less. Beginning with the deeply cupped petals, full them around the center, inside of the cup inward and the tops of the petals 1 inch above the center. Arrange each row between those of the preceding row. (Fig. 35.) Place the calyx strip around the outside, the light green inward and the ends extending out as far as the last row of petals. Fasten with a 15-inch strip of No. 9 wire. (Gen. Instr. No. 6a.) Wrap base and stem with a ¾ inch wide strip of leaf green, adding No. 9 wire to make the stem as long as desired. (Gen. Instr. Nos. 3 and 7.)

Fig. 35 Arranging the Petals Around the Center

Leaf—Using pattern No. 26 cut two or more leaves, the grain of the paper running across the leaf as indicated by the lines on the pattern. Wrap a 10-inch strip of No. 9 wire three times with a ¾ inch wide strip of leaf green. Paste one end of the wrapped wire *across the grain* of the leaf at the center. (Fig. 36.) Brush with paste around the edges and over the pasted wire and place a second leaf on top.

Bud—A bud may be made with 3 petals and 2 calyxes, with or without a center padding of white crepe paper. Make it in the same way as the hollyhock bud. (Fig. 39.)

ℋollyhock

A list of materials required is on page 34

SELECT colors from list given on page 36. Use Nos. 61 or 63 Amber for the center, No. 45 Moss Green for the buds, calyxes, leaves and stem wrapping, Nos. 9 and 15 wire and a dowel or flag stick when a long heavy stalk is desired.

Center—Cut a strip of No. 9 wire 10 inches long. Bend 2 inches back into a loop. Cut a strip of amber crepe paper 1½ inches wide and 20 inches long. Stretch, and wrap around the loop end over and over closely and smoothly Fasten with paste. (Fig. 37.)

Petals—Cut a strip of 5 petals for each flower (pattern No. 17). (Gen. Instr. Nos. 1 and 8.) Cup the petals. (Gen. Instr. No. 4.) Full them evenly around the center in one row, the top of the center just below the edge of the petal. Fasten with a short piece of spool wire, cutting the surplus paper into a pointed base. (Gen. Instr. No. 6a.) (Fig. 38.) Wrap the stem with a ½ inch wide strip of green paper. Make from 5 to 15 flowers for each stalk.

Buds—Make 2 or 3 balls about ½ inch in diameter, of green crepe paper. With pattern No. 18 cut a strip of calyxes. Brush the ball with paste and fasten a strip of 2 or 3 calyxes over the ball, the ends meeting at the top. In the same way, make 4 or more slightly larger buds the color of the flowers, using only 2 calyxes, thus allowing the color to show. Cut the surplus paper into a point and wrap down two inches with a ½ inch wide strip of green crepe. (Gen. Instr. No. 3.) It will not be necessary to use wire for the bud stems. (Fig. 39.)

Assembling—Wrap the No. 15 wire with a 3 inch wide strip of green crepe paper, inserting the green buds at the top and on opposite sides close to the stem. Place the colored buds next, in the same manner, one inch apart; and then the blossoms an inch or more away from the stem and almost touching each other.

Small leaves (pattern No. 19) may be placed here and there between the blossoms. (Gen. Instr. No. 5.) Next place four or more large leaves (pattern No. 20) in the stem wrapping, close to and opposite each other. Add the dowel at this point if used, wrapping it in securely.

Fig. 37

Fig. 39

Fig. 38

Fig. 42

Fig. 40a

Fig. 40b

Morning Glory

A list of materials required is on page 34

THE various colors in which Morning Glories may be made will be found on page 36. Use No. 45 Moss Green for the leaves and stem wrapping, with No. 9 and spool wire.

Petals—Cut petals according to pattern No. 21. (Gen. Instr. No. 1, page 31). Paste the two slanting edges together, one on top of the other, sheen side out. (Fig. 40a.) Trim the wide or top edge evenly all around. (Fig. 40b.) Stretch this edge and roll it back slightly. Gather the petal 1 inch up from the bottom and fasten with a 7-inch strip of spool wire (Gen. Instr. No. 6a), leaving a single stem wire. With a little paste, attach a calyx (pattern No. 22), points upward, so as to cover the fastening wire. Wrap the stem with a ¼ inch wide strip of the green crepe. (Gen. Instr. No. 3.)

Bud—Cut, paste, and trim a petal the same as for the flower. Brush with paste on the inside wide edge and gather together tightly at the top. Gather the bottom edge also without pasting (Fig. 41a); fasten with an 8-inch strip of spool wire, attach a calyx as to the flower and wrap with the ¼ inch wide strip of green. (Fig. 41b.)

Leaves—Cut leaves by pattern No. 23, either *with* or *across the grain*, and wire them (Gen. Instr. No. 10), using 7-inch No. 9 wires.

Assembling—Assemble on a full length No. 9 wire, using a ½ inch wide strip of green for wrapping the stem. First insert a bud stem in the wrapping, exposing 2 inches of its short stem. Then add leaves, buds, and blossoms about 2 inches apart on opposite sides of the stem, each small stem standing out from the main stem 2 inches or more. (Fig. 42.)

Tinting—The inside and outside of the blossom may be tinted with harmonizing colors, and the outside of the bud as well. (Gen. Instr. No. 11.)

Fig. 41a   Fig. 41b   Morning Glory Blossom and Bud

Bachelor's Button

A list of materials required is on page 34

SEE page 36 for colors of Bachelor's Buttons. Use No. 11 White and No. 12 Black for the centers, and No. 45 Moss Green Crepe Paper for leaves and stem.

Center—Cut *across the grain* strips of No. 11 White and No. 12 Black Crepe Paper, 1½ inches wide by 2 inches long. Lay one on top of the other and cut a fringe ½ inch deep. (Gen. Instr. No. 12, page 33.) Roll together evenly, and fasten with paste. (Fig. 43.)

Petals—Cut a strip of 16 petals (pattern No. 27). (Gen. Instr. Nos. 1 and 8.) Twist the lobe of each petal twice, keeping the end flat. (Fig. 44.) Gather the strip ⅝ inch from the bottom, evenly in one row around the center. Fasten with a 10-inch strip of spool wire. (Gen. Instr. No. 6a.) Press the petals out at right angles to the center, and brush out the center a little if necessary. Add 1 or 2 No. 9 wires for the stem which should be from 12 to 18 inches long. (Gen. Instr. No. 7.) Wrap the stem with a ¾ inch wide strip of No. 45 Moss Green Crepe Paper (Gen. Instr. No. 3) and insert 3 or 4 sprays of leaves (pattern No. 28) two inches apart, the first one 3½ inches down the stem. (Gen. Instr. No. 5.) (Fig. 45.)

Fig. 45

Cosmos

A list of materials required is on page 34

SEE page 36 for the colors of the Cosmos. Make the center with a 3½ inch long strip of No. 61 and of No. 63 Amber Crepe Paper, cut into ¼ inch deep fringe and rolled together evenly. Around this, place one row of No. 12 black fringe slightly higher than the amber. Then place a row of the double amber fringe around the outside, level with the center. (Fig. 46.) Cut a strip of 8 petals (pattern No. 29). (Fig. 47.) Cup them near the top (Gen. Instr. No. 4), and with inside of cup next to the center gather them around the center. Complete the same as the Bachelor's Button. (Fig. 48.)

Fig. 43   Fig. 46

Fig. 48

Fig. 44.   Twisting the Bachelor's Button Petals

Fig. 47

Geranium

A list of materials required is on page 34

FOR colors of Geraniums, see page 36, and use either No. 45 Moss or No. 46 Leaf Green Crepe Paper for leaves and stems.

Petals—Cut petals in strips of four (pattern No. 30). (Gen. Instr. Nos. 1 and 8, pages 31 and 33.) Gather the petals ⅝ inch down. Cut away half of the surplus paper, and with a ½ inch wide strip of the green crepe paper, wrap the base and continue to twist into a stem 2 inches long. (Gen. Instr. No. 3.) Press the four petals out into natural shape. (Fig. 49a.)

Fig. 49a

Buds—Cut a piece of crepe paper, the same color as used for the blossoms, 2 inches square. Double through the center diagonally. Place the left forefinger at the center as in Fig. 50a. Bring the left corner over to the right and around the finger and then the right over to the left and around the outside. (Fig. 50b.) Slip the bud off the finger, wrap it more closely and pinch it together ½ inch below the top. Make a 2-inch stem as for the petals.

Group from 9 to 20 buds, blossoms, or buds and blossoms in a cluster evenly, and starting ¾ of an inch down wrap the stems together with a ¾ inch wide strip of green crepe paper. Add two No. 9 wires, from 6 to 10 inches long. (Gen. Instr. No. 7.) (Fig. 49b.) Insert 3 or more wired leaves (Fig. 51) along the stem (pattern No. 31). (Gen. Instr. Nos. 5 and 10.) Allow the leaf stem to extend out of the main stem 1 inch or more.

Fig. 51

If the geranium is to be displayed as a plant in a flower pot or window box, use No. 78 wire instead of No. 9.

To make quantities of geraniums more quickly, cut a strip of crepe paper 1½ inches wide by 18 inches long, and cut into petals ½ inch wide by 1 inch deep. (Gen. Instr. No. 8.) Cut the corners rounding and twist each petal division across the top, twisting toward you with one hand and away from you with the other. (Fig. 52.) Gather the strip together ½ inch up from the bottom and form a cluster. Fasten with a 10-inch strip of No. 9 wire (Gen. Instr. No. 6a) and wrap with a ¾-inch wide strip of green, completing the same as the first cluster.

Fig. 52

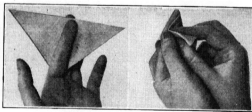

Fig. 49b   Fig. 50a   Fig. 50b

Wisteria

A list of materials required is on page 35

WISTERIA is usually made of No. 23 Purple, No. 22 Violet, and No. 21 Heliotrope Crepe Paper, although for decorative purposes it may also be made in the pinks, blues, or yellows, with either No. 41 Apple or No. 45 Moss Green for leaves and stem wrapping.

Petals—Cut across the grain a 2-inch wide strip of purple, a 2½-inch wide strip of violet, and a 3-inch wide strip of heliotrope crepe paper and stretch each strip fully. For each spray of Wisteria, cut one group of purple petals from pattern No. 32 (Gen. Instr. No. 1, page 31), three of violet from pattern No. 33, and four of heliotrope from pattern No. 34. Twist each petal just below the rounded part, making a complete turn. (Fig. 53.) Put a bit of paste at the center of the straight edge of the purple group. Place the end of a 12-inch strip of green silkateen, crepe paper rope, or spool wire at the pasted spot, and twist the balance of the straight edge around it. (Fig. 54.) In the same way, 1 inch below, paste and fasten a violet group and then the balance of the violet and heliotrope groups, each 1 inch apart.

Fig. 55

Leaves—Cut leaves by pattern No. 35. Start the spray of leaves with one leaf at the end of a 10-inch strip of No. 9 wire. Wrap with a ¾-inch strip of green (Gen. Instr. No. 3), inserting 5 or 7 leaves in the wrapping, the one at the end and the balance 3 inches apart, in pairs, on opposite sides of the stem. (Gen. Instr. No. 5.) Join the sprays of leaves and blossoms on a main stem of No. 9 wire, wrapping with an inch wide strip of green and leaving from 2 to 4 inches of the blossom stem exposed. (Fig. 55.)

Fig. 54

"MILE-A-MINUTE" WISTERIA—Instead of the twisted petals, for decorative purposes the "Mile-a-minute" can be made very quickly. Cut ⅝-inch wide strips of purple, violet, or heliotrope crepe paper through the entire fold, and before unfolding, flute both edges. (Fig. 56.) (Gen. Instr. No. 2.) Loop the strip together in irregular lengths, not longer than 12 inches. Fasten with a 5-inch strip of spool wire. (Gen. Instr. No. 6a.) Wrap the wire with a ½ inch wide strip of green and finish as above. (Fig. 57.)

Fig. 56

Fig. 53 Twisting Petals

Fig. 57

Chrysanthemum

A list of materials required is on page 35

CHRYSANTHEMUMS may be made of single or double strips of petals—see page 36 for colors.

Center—Cut a strip of the crepe paper same as used for petals, 4 inches wide by 15 inches long. (With double petals, use a 7½-inch strip of each color.) Stretch fully, and cut a fringe 1½ inches deep. (Gen. Instr. No. 12, page 33.) Gather and roll the strip, fastening securely with paste. (Fig. 58.)

Petals—For double petals, cut a strip of each shade 5 inches wide and 48 inches long. Paste along one edge (several inches at a time); place one strip on top of the other, evenly, and press together along the pasted edge. STRETCH FULLY. Fold *with the grain* to 8 thicknesses. Pin along the unpasted edge. Trim the pasted edge evenly and cut down from this edge ½ inch wide petals, 2½ inches deep. (Gen. Instr. No. 8.) Shape the ends after pattern No. 36.

To curl the petals use a small cushion of felt or toweling, and a wooden curler (the blunt end of a penholder will do). Place an end of the strip on the cushion, the darker shade up. Hold the curler as shown in Fig. 59, and starting at the top of the petal press the curler firmly down along the petal, and at the same time, with the left hand, lift the cushion and press it against the curler, following the motion of the curler with the lifted cushion. When all petals are curled, cut 12 inches off the end of the strip for the outside row.

Full the long strip around the fringed center, the curled ends inward. Then full the 12-inch strip around the outside, the curled ends outward. Fasten on opposite sides with two 15-inch strips of No. 9 wire. (Gen. Instr. No. 6b.) (Fig. 60.) Cut surplus paper within ¾ of an inch. Attach a calyx (pattern No. 37) (Fig. 61) and starting below the flower base, wrap the stem with a 2-inch wide strip of green crepe paper. (Gen. Instr. No. 3.) Add three No. 78 wires 3 inches apart and insert on opposite sides of the stem, 3 inches apart, 3 leaves made from pattern No. 38, and wired. (Gen. Instr. Nos. 5 and 7.)

Fig. 58

Fig. 60

Fig. 59. Curling Petals

Fig. 61

Easter Lily

A list of materials required is on page 35

CENTER—Cut 6 pieces of green spool wire, each 5 inches long. Wrap the end of one strip down 1 inch with a ½ inch wide strip of No. 41 Apple Green Crepe Paper. (Gen. Instr. No. 3, page 31.) Bend this wrapped end in the center, closely, into a loop, and wrap the loop over and over 10 times or more, forming a smooth, oblong shaped pistil. Wrap the other 5 wires three times, 1 inch down, with a ½-inch wide strip of No. 61 Light Amber Crepe Paper, and fasten with paste. Arrange the green pistil in the center of the 5 stamens, the pistil slightly lower than the stamens, and wrap all together at the base with a short piece of crepe paper. (Fig. 62.)

Petals—Using pattern No. 39, cut a strip of six petals from No. 11 White Crepe Paper, placing the dotted line of the pattern on a fold of the paper. (Gen. Instr. Nos. 1 and 8.) Wire each petal with No. 10 white wire. (Gen. Instr. No. 10.) (Fig. 63.) With the wires on the outside, paste the two slanting edges together, one on top of the other. (Fig. 64.) Curve the wired petals backward and place the center inside the tube of petals, the tops of the stamens coming just below the end of the petal divisions. Full the lily 1 inch up from the bottom and fasten with a 10-inch strip of spool wire. (Fig. 65.) (Gen. Instr. No. 6a.)

Bud—Cut *across the grain* a piece of the white crepe paper 4¼ inches wide by 4 inches long. Paste together the 4¼ inch edges, one on top of the other. Brush a little paste on the inside of one end and gather it closely. Gather the other end without pasting, and fasten with a 16-inch strip of No. 10 white wire. (Fig. 66.) Wrap the stem with a 1¼ inch wide strip of No. 45 Moss Green Crepe Paper, and insert two leaves (pattern No. 40) 4 inches down on opposite sides of the stem. (Gen. Instr. No. 5.) Wrap the lily stem in the same manner, adding No. 10 and No. 78 wires (Gen. Instr. No. 7), inserting the bud stem about 5 inches down, and leaves, in twos, on opposite sides of the stem, which stem should be about 20 inches long. Bend the lily and the bud forward, and press the lily out from the inside to shape it. (Fig. 67.)

Fig. 62

Fig. 65

Fig. 67

Fig. 63   Fig. 64   Fig. 66

Poinsettia

A list of materials required is on page 35

POINSETTIAS may be made of separate petals of No. 81 Red Crepe Paper wired with No. 8 red wire, or with strips of petals unwired. Use Dennison's ready-made centers, or centers of fringed crepe paper.

Wired Petals—For each flower cut two petals (pattern No. 41), four petals (pattern No. 42), and seven petals (pattern No. 43). (Gen. Instr. No. 1, page 31.) Wire each petal on the sheen side. (Gen. Instr. No. 10.)

Center—Cut 5 or 6 ready-made centers in the middle. Place from 8 to 10 of these ends evenly together with three pointed strips of red crepe paper cut ¼ inch wide by 3 inches long (Fig. No. 68), using a 10-inch strip of green spool wire for fastening. (Gen. Instr. No. 6a.)

For the fringed center, cut strips of No. 45 Moss Green and No. 63 Dark Amber Crepe Paper, *across the grain*, 2 inches wide by 8 inches long (slightly stretched). Cut a fringe ¾ inch deep (Gen. Instr. No. 12) and gather the two strips closely, mixing in 3 strips of the red and fastening as above. (Fig. 69.)

Assembling—First place the two small petals (Fig. 70) on opposite sides of the center, wired side underneath, the tips 2¼ inches higher than the center (Fig. 71); then place the four medium sized ones (Fig. 72) and lastly the large petals (Fig. 73), the tips of each group about 2 inches higher than the preceding ones. Fasten with a 10-inch strip of spool wire. Add a No. 78 wire and wrap the stem with a 1¼ inch wide strip of green crepe paper inserting leaves 3 inches apart (pattern No. 44). (Gen. Instr. Nos. 3, 5 and 7.) (Fig. 74.)

Unwired Petals—Cut a strip of 4 petals (pattern No. 45), a strip of 6 petals (pattern No. 46), and a strip of 8 petals (pattern No. 47). (Gen. Instr. Nos. 1 and 8.) Gather the strip of small petals, at the end of the petal divisions, evenly around the center, then the 6-petal strip, and the 8-petal strip, each row 1½ inches higher than the preceding row. Finish as above. (Fig. 75.)

Shaping—Bend the petals away from the center, making a flat open flower. Curve the ends slightly, and cup the leaves toward the stem. (Gen. Instr. No. 4.)

Fig. 74

Fig. 75

Fig. 68   Fig. 69

Fig. 70 Fig. 72   Fig. 73

Fig. 71.   First Two Wired Petals Placed

Carnation

For colors of carnations, see page 36
A list of materials required is on page 35

PETALS—Cut 5 petals for each flower (pattern No. 48) (Gen. Instr. No. 1, page 31), pinning the pattern to the paper before cutting the petals. (Fig. 76.) Picot the outside edges and make five ⅜ inch cuts in each petal as indicated on the pattern. Plait the petals across once through the center, and once lengthwise, to relieve their plainness. (Fig. 77.) Mark the center of the petals with a pin point, and then separate them. Gather each circle of petals together in a cluster from the center up, and twist to hold in place. (Fig. 78.)

Assembling—Arrange 5 clusters together evenly, and, without cutting away any of the surplus paper, fasten with a 10-inch strip of No. 9 wire; fasten the wire again on the opposite side and then underneath, making an oblong shaped base. (Fig. 79.) (Gen. Instr. No. 6a.) Brush this base all around with paste and attach a calyx of No. 45 Moss Green Crepe Paper (pattern No. 49), the points extending out and close under the petals. (Fig. 80.) Beginning one inch below the top of the calyx, wrap the stem with a ¾-inch strip of No. 45 Moss Green Crepe Paper. (Gen. Instr. No. 3.) Add two 15-inch No. 9 wires (Gen. Instr. No. 7) and about 2½ inches down the stem place the first leaf (pattern No. 50), bending and inserting it at the center so the two ends will come out of the stem. (Gen. Instr. No. 5.) Add 5 or 6 other leaves 2½ inches apart, and add two more wires long enough to reach to the end of those already placed. Curl the leaves outward over a blade. (Gen. Instr. No. 9a.)

Fig. 78   Fig. 79

Shaping—Pull the petals out here and there and down to give a natural round, evenly shaped carnation.

Fig. 80

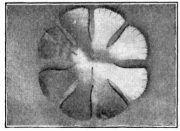

Fig. 76

Fig. 77

Sweetheart Rose

For colors of the Sweetheart Rose, see page 36

A list of materials required is on page 35

CUT a strip of crepe paper 2 inches wide by 4 inches long and divide into a strip of 8 petals ½ inch wide by 1½ inches deep. (Gen. Instr. No. 8, page 33.) Do not round off the corners of the petals. Cup the four right-hand petals outward near the top. (Gen. Instr. No. 4.) Curl the other four petals on the side tops outward over a fine knitting needle, and cup them outward generously. (Fig. 86.) (Gen. Instr. No. 9b.) Fold in the sides of the end cupped petal, making it as near cone shape as possible. Full the second petal around it, evenly, ½ inch from the top, and then the third and fourth. Full the fifth and remaining petals around, placing them slightly higher than the first four, each one overlapping the preceding one. Fasten with a 10-inch strip of spool wire. (Gen. Instr. No. 6a.) Paste a calyx (pattern No. 63) cut from No. 41 Apple Green Crepe Paper, around the base, the points extending up nearly to the top of the petals. Wrap the short stem with a ½ inch wide strip of Apple Green Crepe Paper. (Gen. Instr. No. 3.) (Fig. 87.)

Fig. 87

Rolled Roses

ANOTHER very simple way to make small roses for boutonnieres or to decorate favors is to use a strip of crepe paper 4 inches wide and 6 inches long, the grain of the crepe the 6-inch way. Roll *with the grain* around a steel knitting needle and push the paper together as tightly as possible. (Fig. 88.) Slip off the needle, then unroll the paper about two inches. Roll up again quite loosely and cut off a piece about an inch long. Fasten with a piece of spool wire (Fig. 89) and finish with a calyx and stem, wrapping just as described for the Sweetheart Rose. The materials required will be the same as for the Sweetheart Rose.

Fig. 88

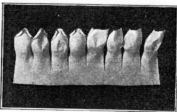

Fig. 86

Columbia Rose

A list of materials required is on page 35

THE rose petals are made with No. 11 White and No. 33 Dark Blush Pink Crepe Paper, and the calyx with No. 41 Apple and No. 45 Moss Green Crepe Paper.

Center—Make a 2-inch long bud, similar to the geranium bud (page 16), using a 4-inch square of the pink crepe paper fully stretched. (Fig. 93.)

Petals—Cut 12 single petals of the pink and 8 double petals of the white and pink (pattern No. 57). (Gen. Instr. No. 1, page 31.) Cup 8 single petals deeply, at the top, 4 at a time. (Fig. 94.) (Gen. Instr. No. 4.) Curl 4 single petals over a blade and cup them generously. (Fig. 95.) (Gen. Instr. No. 9a.) Brush the rounded edges of the double petals with paste, so they will hold together. Curl each double petal over a blade, the pink always under the curl. Curl three again around the top, and cup medium. (Fig. 96.) Curl three others on top sides over a knitting needle and cup a little less. (Fig. 97.) (Gen. Instr. No. 9b.) Curl the two remaining on top sides over a knitting needle, and cup scantily. (Fig. 98.)

Leaves—Use Dennison's No. 3 leaves, or make sprays by fulling one large leaf (pattern No. 58) at the base, placing the end of an 8-inch strip of green spool wire in the fullness and wrapping the end of the leaf and the stem with a ½-inch strip of No. 45 Moss Green Crepe Paper. (Gen. Instr. No. 3.) Insert two of the smaller leaves (pattern No. 59) on opposite sides 1½ inches down. (Gen. Instr. No. 5.)

Using the bud as a center, full the petals one at a time around in the order in which they were prepared, the inside of the cup always toward the center. Keep the top open and place each row of petals slightly higher than the preceding row. Do not force the petals close together. Allow them to fall into natural position. Fasten with a 10-inch strip of spool wire. (Gen.

(Cont'd on page 30)

Fig. 93

Fig. 94

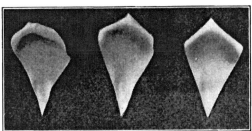

Fig. 95   Fig. 96   Fig. 97

Fig. 98

Fig. 107

American Beauty Rose

A list of materials required is on page 35

THE rose petals are made with No. 35 Cerise and No. 33 Dark Blush Pink Crepe Paper.

Center—Bend about 3 dozen rose stamens in the middle, making a bunch of 6 dozen ends. Fasten with a 3-inch strip of spool wire. (Gen. Instr. No. 6a, page 32.)

Petals—Cut 13 single petals of the cerise (pattern No. 61) (Gen. Instr. No. 1) and 5 double petals of the cerise and pink. (See instructions for double petals under Columbia Rose, page 23.) Cup 3 single petals deeply at the top (Gen. Instr. No. 4), curl the top edges forward over a knitting needle, and crush the edges together. (Gen. Instr. No. 9b.) (Fig. 99.) Flute 6 single petals once at the top (Gen. Instr. No. 2) and cup deeply. (Fig. 100.) Curl 4 on top sides over a blade and cup medium. (Gen. Instr. No. 9a.) (Fig. 101.) Curl 4 double petals over a knitting needle on the top sides, the pink under the curl, and cup very little. (Fig. 102.) Curl the one remaining petal generously on top sides, and cup outward ⅓ inch down and inward ⅔ inch down.

Full the petals around the center one at a time in the order in which they were prepared, the inside of the cupped petals to the inside of the flower. Place the three crushed petals first, slightly higher than the stamen center and full them in one inch from the top. (Fig. 103.) Place each row slightly higher than the preceding one and full the petals a little lower. (Fig. 104.) Like the Columbia Rose, allow the petals to stand out. Do not force them close together. (Fig. 105.) Fasten on

Fig. 100

Fig. 101

Fig. 104.   Placing the Fluted Petals

opposite sides with two 10-inch strips of spool wire. (Gen. Instr. No. 6b.) Attach a single calyx of No. 45 Moss Green Crepe Paper (pattern No. 62) and wrap the stem with a 1¼ inch wide strip of the same color green (Gen. Instr. No. 3), inserting two sprays of Dennison's No. 3 ready-made leaves (Gen. Instr. No. 5) or make the sprays of No. 45 Moss Green Crepe Paper, following instructions under Columbia Rose, page 23. Add three No. 9 wires along the stem, and a No. 78 wire of the desired length. (Gen. Instr. No. 7.) (Fig. 106.)

Fig. 106

The American Beauty Rose may also be made of 12 single and 5 double petals (pattern No. 63), without the stamen center. Cup 7 single petals fully at the top; curl 5 single petals over a blade, and cup them medium; curl the top sides of the 5 double petals, and cup them, each one a little less.

Fig. 102

In assembling the rose, take for the center one of the fully cupped single petals, fold the two sides to the center and make a cone-shaped petal. Around this, assemble the petals in the order in which they were prepared. Complete with calyx, leaves, and stem, as for the open, or full blown rose. (Fig. 107.)

This is called a half blown rose, The beauty of this rose depends largely upon the center which has not fully opened.

It must be kept slightly open at the center, but the petals must be placed so that the inside ones will lie closely at the top and so they will gradually separate toward the outside.

Fig. 99

When making roses for the first time, it will be helpful to have a natural rose before you to study the position taken by the petals, or, if it is impossible to have a natural rose, study the illustrations given, carefully, and try to place the petals as nearly like those shown as possible.

Fig. 105. Placing the Last Double Petal

Fig. 103

Wild Rose

A list of materials required is on page 35

FOR a Wild Rose of single petals use No. 31 Light Blush Pink Crepe Paper; and for one with double petals use No. 11 White with Light Blush Pink, or No. 31 Light with No. 33 Dark Blush Pink, placing the lighter shade toward the center. To prepare double petals, see instructions for the Apple Blossom, page 27.

Center—Make a ball ¼ inch in diameter, and stretch over it a 2-inch square of No. 41 Apple Green Crepe Paper. Pinch together underneath. Bend about 15 rose stamens in the middle and arrange them around the ball. They should stand above the ball ½ or ¾ inch. Fasten with a 10-inch strip of spool wire. (Gen. Instr. No. 6a, page 32.) (Fig. 89.)

Petals—Cut five petals for each rose (pattern No. 54). (Gen. Instr. No. 1.) Curl the petals over a knitting needle on the two rounding top sides, the lighter shade under the curl, if two shades are used. (Gen. Instr. No. 9b.) Cup the petals slightly at the center, inside of cup and curl on same side. (Gen. Instr. No. 4.) Full the petals around the center evenly, inside of cup toward the center. (Fig. 90.) Fasten with spool wire, and attach the calyx (pattern No. 55) made of No. 41 Apple Green Crepe Paper. Curl the points of the calyx outward over a blade. (Gen. Instr. No. 9a.)

Bud—The buds are made the same as geranium buds, using a 2½-inch square of No. 33 Dark Blush Pink Crepe Paper. (See page 16.) Attach a calyx to the bud, the same as used for the rose, and paste the points up around the bud. Fasten with a 12-inch strip of spool wire and wrap the stem with a half inch wide strip of No. 45 Moss Green Crepe Paper. (Gen. Instr. No. 3.) (Fig. 91.) Insert one or two double wired leaves in the bud stem (Gen. Instr. Nos. 5 and 10) (pattern No. 56), or use Dennison's No. 6 leaves. Wrap the rose stem with the ½-inch strip of green, and insert the bud stem and one or two leaves along the way. Add one or two No. 9 wires to make the stem as long as desired. (Gen. Instr. No. 7.) (Fig. 92.)

Fig. 92

Fig. 89

Fig. 90.   Placing the Second Petal

Fig. 91

Apple Blossom

A list of materials required is on page 35

Fig. 81

APPLE Blossom petals are made double of No. 11 White and No. 31 Light Blush Pink and the buds of No. 38 Old Rose or of Light Blush Pink.

Petals—Cut across the grain strips of white and of pink crepe paper, 2 inches wide. Place one strip on top of the other, and paste them together along one edge. Cut into 5-petal strips (pattern No. 51), placing the petal edge of the pattern to the pasted edge of the double strip. (Gen. Instr. Nos. 1 and 8, pages 31 and 33.) Flute each petal edge in the center once (Gen. Instr. No. 2), and cup each petal slightly ⅛ down, the white to the inside. (Gen. Instr. No. 4.) Bend 5 rose stamens in the middle, and about ¾ inch from the top gather a strip of 5 petals around the stamens, the white toward the center, the stamens standing up about ½ inch. Fasten with a 7-inch strip of spool wire (Gen. Instr. No. 6a) and wrap the stem with a ½-inch strip of No. 41 Apple Green Crepe Paper. (Gen. Instr. No. 3.) (Fig. 81.)

Fig. 82

Bud—Make a ball of pink or rose crepe paper ¼ to ⅜ inch in diameter. Stretch a 1½-inch square piece of the same color smoothly over the ball and pinch it together underneath. Attach a calyx (pattern No. 52) of No. 45 Moss Green Crepe Paper, so that the points come well up around the ball. (Fig. 82.) Cut the surplus paper below the ball from the sides only, leaving a long narrow base. Wrap the base and continue an inch or two below, with a half inch wide strip of No. 41 Apple Green Crepe Paper. It is not necessary to use wire for stems. (Fig. 83.)

Make the leaves double (pattern No. 53), using either No. 41 Green or No. 13 Gray with No. 45 Moss Green Crepe Paper, cupping and placing them in the stem wrapping with the Moss Green next to the stem. (Gen. Instr. Nos. 4 and 5.) Group the blossoms, buds and leaves together in clusters (Fig. 84) and then make into branches, using No. 9 wire and wrapping with No. 72 Brown Crepe Paper. (Fig. 85.)

Fig. 83

Fig. 84. Joining Buds and Blossoms

Fig. 85

Fig. 106

Cellophane Flowers

A list of materials required is on page 35

CELLOPHANE FLOWERS are made in very much the same way as those of crepe paper. There is one feature, however, about Cellophane that is different; it cannot be cupped, fluted or stretched.

Because these flowers are used mostly for decorative purposes, they are often exaggerated in size and modernistic in coloring. They may be made entirely of Cellophane or crepe paper may be used covered on one or both sides with Cellophane. Sealing wax is often used in combination with Cellophane to produce flowers which resemble transparent colored glass. Instructions are given here for several varieties, but other kinds, such as poppies, tulips, cosmos and poinsettias, may be as effectively made.

For flowers such as the stalk of flowers in Figure 106, cut a piece of clear Cellophane 2 inches by 4 inches. For the blossoms at the tip of the stalk cut the material a little narrower. Gather through the center the long way and fasten tightly with a 6-inch piece of No. 5 wire that has had a single black or colored glass bead threaded on it. Place the wire across the gathered Cellophane and twist tightly underneath. Spread out the ends of the Cellophane and paste together to form a circle (Fig. 107). Wrap the stem with a ½ inch wide strip of Nile green crepe paper, Cellophane or with strands of embroidery floss. If this latter material is used, care must be taken to see that the strands lie closely side by side.

After the separate flowers are entirely made, but before they are assembled on the stalk, heat a stick of colored transparent sealing wax until very hot and just ready to drop. Daub the wax quickly on the flower, starting at the center and working toward the edge. Do not cover the flower entirely but allow the wax to go on it irregularly and not at all thickly. Work

Fig. 107

Fig. 108

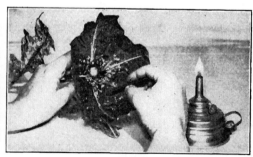

Fig. 109

Fig. 110

quickly and reheat the wax constantly (Fig. 110).
Apply green transparent sealing wax to the leaves.

Leaves — Cut the leaves from clear Cellophane,
using pattern No. 35 but making it about ½ inch
narrower. Wire the leaves with No. 10 wire (Gen.
Instr. No. 10) and apply the wax as described above.

Assembling — Assemble on a 15-inch piece of No. 7
wire, wrapping with either crepe paper, Cellophane
or embroidery floss. If the floss is used the stalk should
be wrapped first with crepe paper. First insert a
flower in the wrapping, exposing 1½ inches of its stem.
Then add blossoms and leaves in whorl formation
(Fig. 108) until 15 flowers and 6 leaves have been
added on the first 8 inches of the stalk.

Poppies are made following the instructions on page
10 but omitting the fluting and cupping of the petals.
The wax is applied to the inside of the petals after the
flower has been entirely assembled (Figs. 109 and 110).

Crepe Paper — and Cellophane Flowers — Con-
ventional flowers such as those shown in Figure 111
are made of crepe paper covered on both sides with
Cellophane. Use ready-made daisy centers. Cover with
glue and sprinkle with silver metallics or cover with
Cellophane, drawing it smoothly over the top of the
center and fastening it tightly underneath close to the
wire stem. Wrap the stem with a ¼ inch wide strip
of Cellophane. Group three centers together and fasten
at the base with a bit of spool wire (Fig. 112). Cut 5
petals (pattern No. 64) from crepe paper the desired
color. Brush all around the edges with mucilage and
place between two pieces of clear Cellophane. Press
down firmly until dry, then trim off the edges evenly
with the crepe paper (Fig. 113). Gather 5 petals about
an inch from the base and arrange evenly spaced
around the group of 3 centers, allowing them to stand
up about 2½ inches (Fig. 114). Complete the flower
the same as for poppies (Fig. 115). Make the leaves of
crepe paper covered on both sides with Cellophane,
having them the same color as flowers or Nile green.

Fig. 111

Fig. 112

Fig. 113

Fig. 115

Fig. 114

Waxed Flowers

ALL kinds of crepe paper flowers may be waxed, although flowers with fairly large petals, like the sweet pea, rose, pond lily, and the like are more attractive than those with many small petals that lie closely together, such as the carnation and aster.

First make the crepe paper flower complete to the last detail including the shaping of the petals. Then assemble

4 lbs. parawax
4 oz. spermaceti
½ plumber's candle

Place the above ingredients in a deep kettle and melt over a slow fire to a temperature of 130 degrees, or, when a piece of crepe paper placed in the liquid and quickly removed will not shrivel up, but will retain a thin transparent coating of the wax. Remove the wick of the candle.

The best results can be obtained when a candy thermometer is used to test the heat.

With the temperature of the liquid at 130 degrees, turn off the heat, and holding the flower by the stem, dip it in the solution, which must be deep enough to cover the flower. Do not keep it there but draw it out quickly and shake it over the kettle so the surplus liquid will drop back in the kettle. Do not allow the liquid to lodge in the center of the flower or between the petals. If it does not drop out with the shaking, remove it gently with the tip of the finger or the end of an orange stick. Separate the petals if they stick together, and before the wax sets reshape them if necessary. When the wax has set sufficiently to hold the flower in the hand (about 10 minutes) dip the stem and leaves in the solution, or if you prefer not to wax the leaves, pour the wax over the stem by spoonfuls. The flower may be re-dipped, two, three or four times, as soon as the wax sets after each dipping, which will be 10 minutes or longer, and for each dipping the temperature of the wax should be slightly lower. It should not be less than 120 degrees at the time of the last dipping. After each dipping place the flower upright so there will be no pressure against it.

If a more glossy finish is desired, break up a stick of transparent amber sealing wax, and dissolve it in enough denatured alcohol to cover it. Allow the waxed flowers to stand 7 hours or more, and then with a small camel's hair brush, paint them with the dissolved sealing wax.

Columbia Rose

(Cont'd from page 23)

Instr. No. 6a.) Attach a double calyx (pattern No. 60), the light green next to the flower. Add three No. 9 wires, 10 inches long (Gen. Instr. No. 7), and wrap the stem with a 1¼ inch wide strip of No. 45 Moss Green Crepe Paper. Add a No. 78 wire and insert 3 or 4 sprays of leaves.

General Instructions

1. Making Patterns and Cutting Crepe Paper by Them

First trace the outline of the pattern on tissue paper, paste the tracing on

Fig. A

cardboard and *cut through all the black lines.* (Fig. A.) This method keeps the pattern sheet intact for cutting new patterns when needed. Cut a strip of crepe paper *across the grain* (unless otherwise directed) ¼ inch or more wider than the pattern, and the desired length. Stretch the strip

Fig. B

slightly. Much time will be saved in cutting if strips are cut through the entire thickness of the fold (Fig. B) or at least long enough to fold into eight thicknesses, in this way cutting for several flowers at one time. Place the pattern on not more than eight thicknesses, from top to base *with the grain* (unless otherwise stated) and cut around all the cut edges of the pattern. (Fig. C.)

2. Fluting

"Flute" means to stretch the paper

slightly across the grain to give a ripple effect. Several thicknesses should be fluted at one time, to secure the soft, ripple effect. Begin at

Fig. C

the left and hold the edges to be fluted between the thumbs and forefingers, the thumbs being not more than ⅛ inch apart.

Push the edges away from you with the left thumb, and pull forward with the right forefinger, and with this motion, stretch the paper slightly between the thumbs and forefingers. *Do not twist it.* (Fig. D.) Move the hands a little to the right, plac-

ing the left forefinger in the ripple just made, and the right in unfluted space, and repeat until the amount desired has been fluted.

Fig. D

3. Wrapping Stems

Stems should be wrapped with a narrow strip of crepe paper, cut *across the grain,* or a wider strip doubled, depending upon the size of the stem. For long, thick stemmed flowers, the strip may be cut one to two inches wide and doubled through the center lengthwise. Single strips ½ or ¾ inch wide are used for the shorter and thinner stems.

Fig. E

Brush a little paste on the end of the folded or the single strip, attach it to the calyx or up close under the flower, stretch and wind the strip around two or three times tightly. Then, holding the stem wire in the right hand, twirl it around and around; at the same time, with the left hand, guide the strip, slanting it down and stretching it so that it will wrap the stem smoothly. (Fig. E.)

Make a neat finish by cutting the strip $\frac{1}{2}$ inch below the end of the stem wire, brushing a little paste on the end of the strip, and fastening it securely by continuing to twirl the stem a few times and pressing firmly with the finger tips. Cut off any ragged end.

4. Cupping

Fig. F

Take several thicknesses of petals or leaves together, or a single one, and with the thumbs in the center of the petal or leaf, and forefingers on the opposite side near the edges, push out into shape. (Fig. F.) After cupping a folded strip of petals, unfold the strip, and reverse the cupping of some of the petals so they will all be cupped the same way.

5. Inserting Leaves in Stems

Fig. G

Wrap the stem up to the point where the leaf is to be inserted, full the leaf at its base, and place it against the stem so that the top edge of the wrapping strip will be at a point on the leaf from $\frac{1}{2}$ to $1\frac{1}{2}$ inches from its base, depending upon the size of the leaf. A small leaf, like the Sweet Pea leaf, need be wrapped in only $\frac{1}{2}$ inch, while a Jonquil leaf should be wrapped in $1\frac{1}{2}$ inches. (Fig. G.) Enclose other leaves on opposite sides of the stem, the required distance apart, and complete the stem wrapping as directed in paragraph No. 3. Sprays of leaves having wired stems may be inserted in the stem wrapping close to the leaf, or the leaves may stand out from the stem one or two inches.

6. Wire Fastenings

(*a*) Place the center (or the end if a single stem is desired) of a strip of wire at the base of the flower, close up under

Fig. H   Fig. I

the petals, and wind it around once, twisting it together closely once or twice at the side, to hold. Cut away the surplus paper below the wire, straight across (unless otherwise directed), leaving about $\frac{1}{2}$ inch for security. For a pointed base, cut the surplus paper at the sides instead of straight across. Bring each strand of wire half way around on opposite sides, and then down, and twist together underneath. (Fig. H.)

(*b*) For a very large flower, use two fastening wires. First, fasten one wire at the side as explained in (*a*), and then place a second wire of the same length, fastening it on the opposite side. Cut away surplus paper, as above, bring the two double strands straight down and fasten together underneath. (Fig. I.)

7. Adding Wire to Lengthen a Stem

Place the wire to be added beside the ones being wrapped, an inch or two above the end, and continue wrapping the stem. Do not twist the wires to-

Fig. J

gether. When several wires are to be added, place each one ½ inch or more below the other.

8. Strips of Petals

The grain of crepe paper should always be from point, or top, to base of

Fig. K

a petal or leaf, *unless definitely stated otherwise.* When petals are to be cut in a strip, first cut the desired width *across the grain,* either through the entire thickness of the fold (using the edge of the packet as a cutting guide) (Fig. B), or cut a shorter length. Stretch slightly, and fold the strip, *with the grain,* to eight thicknesses or less. Make straight cuts down the required distance and the required width apart, and round off each petal division as required. (Fig. J.)

9. (a) Curling with a Blade

Place the end to be curled over a

Fig. L

knife or scissors blade, and holding it between the thumb and blade, draw the blade up and along, pressing lightly with the blade. (Fig. K.)

(b) Curling with a Knitting Needle

Roll the top edges of the petals over a No. 10, 14 or 15 steel knitting needle. (Fig. L.) If a crushed effect is desired, as for the first petals of the American Beauty Rose, roll and push the crepe close together on the needle. (Fig. M.)

Fig. M

10. Wiring Leaves or Petals

Cut as many No. 8 Red, No. 9 Green or No. 10 White Wires as there are leaves or petals to be wired. one inch or more longer than the petal or leaf. Lay the wires together on a paper over a flat surface. Hold down the ends with the finger and brush one side of the wires with paste. Place each one pasted side down, in the center of a petal or leaf, allowing the extra length to project below the base. Press down firmly to dry. (Fig. N.) For a double leaf, paste around the edges and over

Fig. N

the center wire, and attach a second leaf evenly.

11. Tinting

Soak a small piece of paper in a very little water until the color is removed. With a brush, or a small fold of white crepe paper dipped in the liquid, brush the surface that is to be tinted very lightly.

12. Fringing Crepe

Cut a strip of crepe paper *across the grain,* as wide and as long as desired. Stretch fully for a very fine fringe and less for a coarser fringe. Fold the strip in half, *with the grain,* and repeat to not exceeding eight

Fig. O

thicknesses. Cut *with the grain* inward from the edge along the strip, making as close and as deep cuts as desired, leaving ½ inch or more uncut along the opposite edge. (Fig. O.)

Materials Required

Material for 6 Dozen Sweet Peas
Approximate Cost $0.90
1 Fold Crepe Paper for Flowers
1 Fold No. 45 Moss Green Crepe Paper
2 Spools No. 1 White Wire
2 Dozen No. 9 Green Wire (for foliage)

Material for 4 Dozen Jonquils
Approximate Cost $1.40
1 Fold No. 61 Light Amber Crepe Paper
1 Fold No. 63 Dark Amber Crepe Paper
1 Fold No. 45 Moss Green Crepe Paper
1 Fold No. 70 Sand Crepe Paper
2 Spools No. 2 Green Wire
3 Dozen No. 9 Wire

Material for 3 Dozen Tulips
Approximate Cost $1.15
1 Fold Crepe Paper for Flowers
1 Fold No. 12 Black Crepe Paper
1 Fold No. 45 Moss Green Crepe Paper
3 Dozen No. 9 Green Wire
1 Spool No. 2 Green Wire

Material for 10 Dozen Flanders Poppies
Approximate Cost $0.65
1 Fold Crepe Paper for Flowers
1 Fold No. 45 Moss Green Crepe Paper
1 Fold No. 12 Black Crepe Paper
2 Spools No. 2 Green Wire

Material for 3 Dozen Red Poppies
Approximate Cost $1.10
1 Fold No. 81 Red Crepe Paper
1 Fold No. 45 Moss Green Crepe Paper
1 Fold No. 12 Black Crepe Paper
2 Dozen No. 9 Green Wire
2 Spools No. 2 Green Wire

Material for 4 Dozen Daisies
Approximate Cost for White Daisies $0.85;
Black-Eyed Susans $1.00; Marguerites $0.85
White Daisies
1 Fold No. 11 White Crepe Paper
1 Fold No. 63 Dark Amber Crepe Paper
1 Fold No. 45 Moss Green Crepe Paper
2 Spools No. 2 Green Wire
1 Dozen No. 9 Green Wire

Black-Eyed Susans
1 Fold No. 63 Dark Amber Crepe Paper
1 Fold No. 72 Brown Crepe Paper
1 Fold No. 12 Black Crepe Paper
1 Fold No. 45 Moss Green Crepe Paper
2 Spools No. 2 Green Wire
1 Dozen No. 9 Wire

Yellow Marguerites
1 Fold No. 61 Light Amber Crepe Paper
1 Fold No. 63 Dark Amber Crepe Paper
1 Fold No. 45 Moss Green Crepe Paper
2 Spools No. 2 Green Wire
1 Dozen No. 9 Wire

Material for 1 Dozen Pond Lilies
Approximate Cost $0.80
1 Fold Crepe Paper for Petals
1 Fold No. 41 Apple Green Crepe Paper
1 Fold No. 46 Leaf Green Crepe Paper
1 Fold No. 61 Amber Crepe Paper
1 Dozen No. 9 Wire

Material for 1 Dozen Stalks Hollyhocks
Approximate Cost $1.40
1 Fold Crepe Paper for Flowers
1 Fold No. 61 Light Amber Crepe Paper
1 Fold No. 45 Moss Green Crepe Paper
2 Dozen No. 9 Wire
1 Dozen No. 15 Wire
2 Spools No. 2 Green Wire

Material for 3 Dozen Sprays of Morning Glories
Approximate Cost $1.80
1 Fold Crepe Paper for Flowers
1 Fold No. 45 Moss Green Crepe Paper
3 Spools No. 2 Green Wire
6 Dozen No. 9 Wire

Material for 3 Dozen Bachelor's Buttons
Approximate Cost $1.10
1 Fold Crepe Paper for Flowers
1 Fold No. 12 Black Crepe Paper
1 Fold No. 11 White Crepe Paper
1 Fold No. 45 Moss Green Crepe Paper
1 Spool No. 2 Wire
2 Dozen No. 9 Wire

Material for 3 Dozen Cosmos
Approximate Cost $1.25
1 Fold Crepe Paper for Flowers
1 Fold No. 61 Light Amber Crepe Paper
1 Fold No. 63 Dark Amber Crepe Paper
1 Fold No. 12 Black Crepe Paper
1 Fold No. 45 Moss Green Crepe Paper
1 Spool No. 2 Wire
2 Dozen No. 9 Wire

Material for 1 Dozen Sprays of Geraniums
Approximate Cost $0.80
1 Fold Crepe Paper for Flowers
1 Fold No. 45 Moss Green Crepe Paper
1 Dozen No. 9 Wire
1 Dozen No. 78 Wire

cMaterials Required — Continued

Material for 2 Dozen Wisteria
Approximate Cost $1.15

1 Fold No. 21 Heliotrope Crepe Paper
1 Fold No. 22 Violet Crepe Paper
1 Fold No. 23 Purple Crepe Paper
1 Fold No. 45 Moss Green Crepe Paper
2 Dozen No. 9 Green Wire
1 Hank 1/16 in. Crepe Paper Rope

Material for 1 Dozen Chrysanthemums
Approximate Cost $2.05

2 Folds Crepe Paper for Flowers
1 Fold No. 45 Moss Green Crepe Paper
3 Dozen Chrysanthemum Leaves
3 Dozen No. 78 Green Wire
1 Dozen No. 9 Green Wire

Material for 1 Dozen Easter Lilies
Approximate Cost $1.70

1 Fold No. 11 White Crepe Paper
1 Fold No. 61 Light Amber Crepe Paper
1 Fold No. 41 Apple Green Crepe Paper
1 Fold No. 45 Moss Green Crepe Paper
3 Dozen No. 10 Wire
1 Dozen No. 78 Wire
3 Spools No. 2 Green Wire

Material for 1 Dozen Poinsettias
Approximate Cost $1.35

1 Fold No. 81 Red Crepe Paper
1 Fold No. 63 Dark Amber Crepe Paper
1 Fold No. 45 Moss Green Crepe Paper
3 Dozen No. 8 Red Wire
1 Dozen No. 78 Wire
1 Spool No. 2 Wire

Material for 2 Dozen Carnations
Approximate Cost $0.90

1 Fold Crepe Paper for Flowers
1 Fold Moss Green Crepe Paper
3 Dozen No. 9 Wire

Material for 6 Dozen Sweetheart Roses
Approximate Cost $1.40

1 Fold Crepe Paper for Flowers
1 Fold No. 41 Apple Green Crepe Paper
2 Spools No. 1 Wire
6 Dozen No. 6 Rose Leaves

Material for 1 Dozen Columbia Roses
Approximate Cost $1.90

1 Fold No. 11 White Crepe Paper
1 Fold No. 33 Dk. Blush Pink Crepe Paper
1 Fold No. 45 Moss Green Crepe Paper
1 Fold No. 41 Apple Green Crepe Paper
2 Dozen No. 78 Leaves
1 Spool No. 2 Green Wire
1 Dozen No. 78 Wire
1 Dozen No. 9 Wire

Material for 1 Dozen American Beauty Roses
Approximate Cost $2.25

1 Fold No. 35 Cerise Crepe Paper
1 Fold No. 33 Dk. Blush Pink Crepe Paper
1 Fold No. 45 Moss Green Crepe Paper
1 Bunch Rose Stamens
1 Spool No. 2 Wire
1 Dozen No. 78 Wire
1 Dozen No. 9 Wire
3 Dozen Dennison's No. 3 Rose Leaves

Material for 1 Dozen Wild Roses
Approximate Cost $1.45

1 Fold No. 31 Lt. Blush Pink Crepe Paper
1 Fold No. 33 Dk. Blush Pink Crepe Paper
1 Fold No. 41 Apple Green Crepe Paper
1 Fold No. 45 Moss Green Crepe Paper
2 Bunches Dennison's Rose Stamens
3 Dozen No. 6 Rose Leaves
1 Spool No. 2 Green Wire
1 Dozen No. 9 Wire

Material for 2 Dozen Sprays of Apple Blossoms
Approximate Cost $1.70

1 Fold No. 11 White Crepe Paper
1 Fold No. 31 Lt. Blush Pink Crepe Paper
1 Fold No. 13 Gray Crepe Paper
1 Fold No. 45 Moss Green Crepe Paper
1 Fold No. 41 Apple Green Crepe Paper
1 Fold No. 72 Brown Crepe Paper
3 Bunches Rose Stamens
3 Spools No. 1 White Wire
1 Dozen No. 9 Wire

Material for 1 Dozen Cellophane Flowers
Approximate Cost $1.85

1 Roll Clear Cellophane
1 Fold Crepe Paper
1 Spool No. 5 Wire
1 Dozen No. 10 Wire
1 Dozen No. 78 Wire
4 Sticks Transparent Sealing Wax color for flowers
3 Sticks Green Transparent Sealing Wax

Suggested Colors of Dennison Crepe for Various Flowers

Dennison's Crepe Paper is admirably suited to the making of flowers because of its texture and pliability as well as the variety of its colors.

Bachelor's Button

No. 11 white, No. 21 heliotrope, No. 22 violet, No. 23 purple, No. 24 fuchsia, No. 54 French blue, No. 55 bluebird blue, No. 33 blush pink and No. 57 delft blue.

Carnation

No. 11 white, Nos. 31, 32, 32½, 33 and 34 pink, No. 36 salmon, No. 81 red, No. 83 ruby and No. 84 flame.

Chrysanthemum

Single petals—Use any shade of pink, yellow or red; also No. 21 heliotrope, No. 22 violet, No. 23 purple or No. 11 white.

Double petals—

Outside	Inside
No. 83 ruby	with No. 61 amber
No. 21 heliotrope	with No. 22 violet
No. 61 light amber	with No. 11 white
No. 21 heliotrope	with No. 32 pink
No. 31 pink	with No. 33 pink
No. 11 white	with No. 33 pink

Cosmos

No. 11 white, No. 21 heliotrope, No. 22 violet, No. 23 purple, No. 24 fuchsia, Nos. 31, 32, 32½, 33 and 34 pink, No. 35 cerise, No. 81 red and No. 83 ruby.

Flanders Poppy

The shape of the Flanders Poppy is not unlike the small garden poppy, and in addition to its official color, No. 84 flame, it may also be made with Nos. 31, 32, 32½, 33 and 34 pink, No. 21 heliotrope, No. 22 violet, No. 23 purple and No. 81 red.

Geranium

No. 11 white, Nos. 31, 32, 32½, 33 and 34 pink, No. 36 salmon, No. 37 American Beauty, No. 81 red, No. 83 ruby and No. 84 flame.

Hollyhock

No. 11 white, No. 24 fuchsia, Nos. 31, 32, 32½, 33 and 34 pink, No. 36 salmon, No. 37 American Beauty, No. 38 old rose, No. 81 red and No. 83 ruby.

Morning Glory

No. 11 white, No. 21 heliotrope, No. 22 violet, No. 23 purple, No. 24 fuchsia, Nos. 31, 32, 32½, 33 and 34 pink, No. 35 cerise, No. 36 salmon, No. 38 old rose, No. 51 celestial blue, No. 30 shell pink and No. 57 delft blue.

Pond Lily

No. 11 white, No. 31 light blush pink, No. 21 heliotrope and No. 60 primrose.

Sweetheart Rose

No. 11 white, Nos. 31, 32, 32½ and 33 pink, No. 60 primrose, No. 61 light amber and No. 91 apricot.

Sweet Pea

No. 11 white, No. 21 heliotrope, No. 22 violet, No. 23 purple, No. 24 fuchsia, Nos. 30, 31, 32, 32½, 33 and 34 pink, No. 35 cerise, No. 36 salmon, No. 60 primrose, No. 66 sun-glow, No. 84 flame and No. 91 apricot.

Tulip

Single Petals—No. 11 white, Nos. 32, 32½, 33 and 34 pink, No. 36 salmon, No. 38 old rose, Nos. 61 and 63 amber, No. 62 canary, Nos. 64 and 65 orange and Nos. 81 and 84 red.

Double Petals—Always use the darker shade on the inside. No. 33 pink with No. 37 American Beauty; No. 22 violet with No. 23 purple; No. 61 light with No. 63 dark amber; No. 21 heliotrope with No. 22 violet; No. 23 purple with No. 24 fuchsia; No. 31 light with No. 33 dark blush pink; and No. 84 flame with No. 36 salmon.

Lightning Source UK Ltd.
Milton Keynes UK
UKOW03f0321050617
302633UK00001B/7/P